What Will You Say, *God?*

BOBBIE LAVENDER

What Will You Say, God?
Copyright © 2022 by Bobbie Lavender

ISBN: 978-1639452828 (Paperback)
         978-1639452835 (Ebook)

Writers' Branding
1800-608-6550
www.writersbranding.com
orders@writersbranding.com

In memory of my son, Robert Reynaud Lavender,
and my husband, Charles Lavender.

This book is dedicated to my daughter, Robbie Lavender Nichols, my granddaughters, Charlie Elizabeth Nichols and Burkley Grace Nichols, my family, and friends who never gave up on me, and have continued to show their support in these tough and trying times.

The purpose of this book is to help you reflect on your life, and to ask yourself "How did I do?" What experiences have you had? Can you relate to some passages in this book, if so, how did you cope? Hopefully, you will find some encouragement in situations, and become aware of the temptations surrounding you daily. Also, to reveal that others are having the same, or near experiences, and to realize that you are not alone in your struggles for salvation.

What Will You Say God By Bobbie Lavender

What will You say, God,
when I get to heaven?
What will You say?
Did I do a good job?
Did I fight a good battle?
What will You say, God?

Did I weather the storm well?
Did I ride the waves?
Did I pass the test?
Did I love GOOD and hate EVIL?
When I should have, did I walk away?
What will You say, God?

Only You, dear God,
can find all the little shredded pieces of my heart,
and mend them together again.
Only You, God, can cure the pain.
What will You say, God?

Did I help when, and where I could?
Did I care, or did I forget your Word?
What will You say, God?

Did I show that I loved You to others,
through my actions and my deeds?
Did I do enough to please?
What will You say, God?

Did I do things for your glory,
or did I take things for granted?

Bobbie Lavender

Did I leave the world a better place,
or did I mark its face?
What will You say, God?

Did I try hard enough?
Did I thank You enough?
Did I lead the way for others
to follow every day?
What will You say, God?

Did I follow the rules?
Did I love, trust, endure and obey?
Was I strong or weak?
What will You say when you speak?
What will You say, God?

When I was scared, did I call on your name?
When I was lost, did I pray?
When I walked the dark streets at night,
did I seek your hand?
Did I rely on Your might?
What will You say, God?

If You show me, will I see?
If You hold my hand,
and walk with me, will I know?
If You call me, will I hear?
Will I feel You near?
What will You say, God?

Did I carry the load? Did I do my best?
Did I count my blessings,
or did I swindle my life away?
What will you say, God?

I come before You,
naked as the day I was born.
I surrender all.
Will I walk the streets of gold,
or will I suffer and mourn?
What will You say, God?
What will You say?

Only You know my heart.
Only You know the whole story of my life.
Did I make it?
Did I accomplish the things that You had planned for me,
or did I ignore the opportunities?
What will You say, God?

And when the devil came, did I say,
"Please come in, have a seat and stay,"
or did I say, "GO AWAY"?
Did I walk the road of righteousness,
or did I always sway?
What will You say, God?

When the winds blew hard,
and the hail was heavy, did I bold up,
and face the feat, or did I shrink into a ball,
and shrivel away?
What will You say, God?

How many times did I not recognize your gifts?
How many times did I misuse your gifts?
You, who made me so perfect, and gave me everything.
How many times have I sinned?
How could you love me?
What will You say, God?

Forgive me God, for at the time,
I did not think; I did not care.
I let the wind blow through my hair,
and the devil was my playmate.
I know that You forgive,
and wash us white as snow.
How You love so deeply, I do not know.
What will You say, God?

I am so honored to be your child.
I am so blessed to have You as my heavenly Father.
What more could I ask?
What blessing could be greater?
For the love of God, have mercy on me,
my loving God, my merciful savior.
What will You say, God?

Did I measure up, or did I fall down?
When I missed the mark, did you frown?
Did I meet and conquer my adversaries,
or did I back away?
What will You say, God?

Did I play a fair game, or did I cheat?
What's my score?
Is it high or low or just in between?
Where do I stand?
Will I weep?
Can I shout, "Hallelujah,"
and "Praise be to God"?
Will the sun shine?
Will it be a glorious day?
What will You say, God?

Did I praise your name on the dawn of each new day?
Did I sing loudly and clearly to proclaim your greatness?

When You called, was I willing to obey?
What will You say, God?

And how many people did I hurt along the way?
Did I not know right from wrong?
Was it something that I did?
Was it something that I said?
I did not consider the consequences that I must pay.
Oh, dear God! -
What will You say, God?

Did I ask too much?
Did I give enough?
It's too late in the day to turn back now.
My only hope is to repent, and be forgiven.
I must reminisce about the past,
learn from my mistakes,
and pray for strength from above to move forward with faith,
endurance, and determination to honor and please my God.
Oh, God.
What will You say, God?

Forgive me of shady thoughts that entered my mind.
Of all the knowledge that I have obtained,
how could I go astray?
What will You say, God?

What a privilege to come to earth to work and play.
Did I do my best? Did I pass the test?
I hope I did; I do pray.
What will You say, God?

Did I bear the load?
Did I care for the animals, the old and weak?
Did I teach my knowledge to others, so they could reap?
What will You say, God?

Did I share my blessings of talents and wealth with all my might,
or was I envious and jealous of others' delight?
Did I lie or steal or bring discord among my clan, day or night?
What will be my plight?
And with your hands that worked and formed with clay...
did I bring joy, or did I permit rust and decay?
What will You say, God?

Was I loving and forgiving of others' faults,
or was I impatient and haughty,
and just through them to be unclean,
deplorable, and naughty?
What will You say, God?

It was easy to be bad;
but hard to be right.
What road did I take?
Was I consistent in my choices?
Were You always on my mind?
Were You always in sight?
Was I asleep, or was I awake?
Did I cheat to get the answers,
or was I willing to exert effort and explore?
Was I trustworthy, reliable, and noble in my choices
and relationships that I experienced here on earth?
Was I an example to follow, or a character of low repute?
Do I have a chance?
Can I still contribute?
What will You say, God?

Of all the many choices I made,
were they a delight in your sight?
Did I put a smile on your face,
or a tear in your eye?
Judge me mercifully, here I am.
What will You say, God?

Oh God, in my humble way,
may I have served you to the ultimate.
My I have cherished my privilege
of living on earth to glorify You,
and when I return home to your magnificent kingdom,
may I have proven to be a worthy servant?
What will You say, God?

Of all the things I've read and know,
of all the things I've seen here below,
they don't release me of my responsibilities.
In fact, they increase them just that much more.
The more I get, the more I owe.
Oh, God
What will You say, God?

And when God ask,
"Where have you been?"
"Whom have you seen?"
A smile I can put on my face,
for I have been in the right place.
My associates, I chose with care.
I do not want to entertain the devil's host.
It's just me, the Father,
the Son, and the Holy Ghost.
It is these I chose. God,
I don't have time to lose.
I have to do the most.
What will You say, God?

When things get "tuff,"
and I get stuck in the mud,
why can't I immediately go into overdrive?
Why do I sit and spin and spin?
Why do I cry and cry?
That's no way to win.

Bobbie Lavender

"Do what I can."
This my motto should be,
and on the rest, God depend.
And when I'm at my row's end,
can I turn and see where I've been?
Don't get caught up in the mire.
Remember, the devil is waiting,
he has an evil desire.
Don't fall for his lie.
It is only God, with whom you can fully rely.
What will You say, God?

When I sit and contemplate,
I stand in awe of the mysteries,
the marvels and the magnitude of life's conception.
It is hard to conceive,
it is hard to relate,
but don't forget,
I am a child of God,
a child of faith.
For God's call, I will patiently wait.
What will You say, God?

Oh God, You have given me so much;
it's inconceivable, it blows my mind.
I try diligently each and every day
to remember the rules of a righteous life,
and be mindful of what is at stake.
And at the dawn of each new day,
and at the end of my prayer,
I highly phrase your name forever more.
There is no room for any mistake.
What will You say, God?

Mine is instant gratification.
Well, that's not how it is.

That's not the ultimate treasure.
Don't you recall?
It's not about your pleasure,
but to please God above all measure.
Why are you here... to party and have fun?
No, it's about love to God above
and to receive His acceptation of love.
Oh, little one, did you pass the test of time?
Did you hear the bells of heaven chime?
What a glorious day, let it be, let it be.
What will You say, God?

And don't you think the time
won't come when you will be accountable.
All your choices will be displayed in full view, on the table.
Please God, wash away those black spots,
make them clean, let no evidence be seen.
What will You say, God?

Dear God you know,
I have never been an advocate for change.
I like things to remain the same.
But of course, nothing does,
we would become stagnant and growth would be slow.
We wouldn't get to see the seasons,
smell the roses, dance in the breezes,
hear the birds chirrup, or the bees buzz.
God, You planned everything just perfectly.
What will You say, God?

Did I regress, or did I progress?
How many times did I fall?
How many times did You reach far down and pull me up?
I was covered with mud and tar,
and You cleanse me as bright as the morning star.
I love You so. I am so glad You are who You are....

a never changing rock, the Alpha and the Omega;
the first, the last.
Not wishy nor washy,
but steadfast in focus,
steadfast in love.
God, from the bottom of my heart,
Thank You for protecting me.
Thank You for taking care of me.
Thank you for quenching my fears in all I do.
No love do I put before You.
Help me also to be steadfast in all I do,
to come to my heavenly home and collect my due.
Oh God, I can hardly wait to be there with You.
What will You say, God?

If you can't give with love in your heart,
and with your 10%,
you cannot depart,
then you are far from heaven bound.
You are a thief...
taking what is not yours
and expecting happiness and relief.
Oh, what a horrible thing,
what a shame,
and then you have the audacity to call on His name.
Oh, you are so shallow and small,
greedy and spoiled, and to think of all your efforts and toils.
How hard you did work, and all for naught.
What will You say, God?

Oh God, I stand in awe of your magnificent creation.
You are a fantastic mathematician.
Everything works in perfect unification,
from the smallest minute cell,
to the enormous solar system.
Everything has its place,

even the things we see,
and the things invisible.
How do You do it?
What is your secret?
My brain just won't comprehend,
but I do know that on You,
I can depend.
I love you, You are my friend.
What will You say, God?

When I lost my love,
a dagger was shot into my heart.
It stung and it burned,
and took my will to live away.
It was a dark and glumly day.
What choice did I have?
I had to struggle on.
You did not say that the roses would always bloom.
There is no discretion;
in the end, all of us must face the tomb.
For all the millions, will there be enough room?
And tell me Lord, just how large is heaven?
What will You say God?

There is certainly a magnitude of variety.
Tell me, why is the bunny's fur so soft,
and the turtle's shell so hard?
And why don't they have a house?
Why do they roam around in the yard,
and contend with anxiety?
For each of us to survive,
You gave the necessary measure.
Did I use my gift wisely,
or did I consume them foolishly;
and when the trumpets blow,
will I know it is time go?

Just hold my hand,
everything will be grand,
I will try to understand.
What will You say, God?

"God don't like ugly."
Watch how you treat your neighbor.
You will be held accountable.
The decree is written in stone.
"Love your neighbor as yourself."
You simply cannot bring dirt to the table.
God has His rules,
and for all of them there is a reason,
all things have a season.
I know that I should not ask WHY,
for now, God will not reply.
Wash me as white as snow,
and I will be with you in heaven forever more.
Oh, what joy it is to know that,
I will be with my family, and my friends,
to share love as never before.
What will You say, God?

If You could go back,
and You could,
how many things would You change about creation?
Would You even create,
would that even be your intention?
Are You sorry you did,
or are you glad You did?
Did we measure up to our potential?
Have we satisfied your vision?
We come before You on bended knees,
fully aware of our misgivings.
God, You are all I've got, and actually,
that's more than enough,

certainly more that I deserve,
with all the things that have occurred,
and You know that some things have been most absurd.
What will You say, God?

And when I am asleep at night,
and You are watching over my bed,
may I awake with the early morning light,
and remember to praise your name?
Did I do it?
Was I committed to my mission?
Did I live a good and faithful life,
or was it all in vain?
What will You say, God?

What did I do that was ever great?
Did I meet my mission?
Did I recognize truth,
or did I think it all fiction?
What will You say, God?

If God were to come down,
and speak my name;
if He would grant me just one wish,
what do you think I would proclaim?
I have thought about this for many a time,
and for all the goodly and worthily choices,
"suffering" will not leave my mind.
The thought pierces my heart,
and I always cry.
Oh, Jesus, I can see You now,
on the cross,
sweating blood and suffering for my atonement,
suffering for my sins.
Oh, how I wish that this had never been.
Oh, what a sacrifice,

oh, what a price.
And tell me, God, why do the innocent suffer
why do they bear the pain?
What did they do to hold the banner of shame?
And, again, in my heart,
on the deepest string,
I cannot for the sake of love,
my pain to restrain,
when I visualize the ultimate fear on an animal's face,
as he tries to free himself
from the iron locks on the monstrous trap.
How, dear God, can this be endured?
Yes, God, these, and many more,
are the reasons why I humbly, sincerely,
ask you to eradicate the existence of suffering.
What will You say, God?

Do you remember
the first breath you ever took;
your very first?
It was the action of inhaling,
not exhaling.
God blew in your breath,
and you blew out.
That is the exchange.
That's what life is all about.
Think about this.
Think about the relationship.
The first breath of life,
God gave to you, you inhaled,
and at your life's end, you will exhale.
You will give your breath back
to God from where it did initiate.
It has been a give and take situation,
but at the close, you will give it back,
never again to set the rhythm.

This phenomenon gave me life.
Will I need this occurrence when I get to heaven?
What is in the plan?
I don't understand.
I just know that I want to hold your hand.
What will You say, God?

One thing for sure,
through all my horrors,
you loved me,
you washed away my tears,
and calmed my fears.
Time can do so much.
I was born a dependent baby,
and now I am a dependent old and crippled person.
Where did time go?
It was here today and gone tomorrow.
I had many happy times, and many sorrows.
And when I was young,
and flying up "fool's hill,"
would I have listened, would I
have obeyed your will?
What will You say, God?

Oh, God, forgive me for what I am about to say,
but God, sometimes You seem so far away.
It behooves me, and frustrates me too.
I look and I cannot see, I listen,
but I do not hear.
I touch, but there is nothing to feel.
I can't concentrate;
I have lost the realm of reality.
Sometimes, I feel like I'm in this, all alone.
I'm wondering, how far am I engaged,
and how far do I have to roam?
Come quickly, Lord Jesus Christ,

relieve me of the nauseous separation
devastations.
I believe that only You are in control.
Only You can save my soul.
Lift me up in Your arms,
let me feel the flow of security.
Let me know that there is so much more,
for now is now, but that's only an instant.
My focus should be on heaven, and on this,
I must be very persistent.
What will You say, God?

And when I was shot down,
and squirming on the ground,
You came and found me alive.
You lifted me up, oh so high,
and assured me that life was divine.
What will You say, God?

Did I listen to the birds sing?
Did I play in the brook?
Did I consider the intricate design of each little flower,
or did I even look?
And on my journey home,
will I be in glee?
Will I meet my friends?
Will I know my family?
What will You say, God?

I cannot remember when my life began,
so I do not know when it will end.
I must be careful what I say and where I have been.
When all is said and done,
and there is no more, I,
God, when You knock,
will open the door.

With my arms open wide,
I will let You inside.
A new beginning must begin.
Let it begin with love and pride.
What will You say, God?

Did I proclaim Your name without shame?
Was I true to my character,
or did I always complain?
Life is no joke; time will tell.
Is it heaven, or is it hell?
Your way you must pave, so
be very careful what you crave.
What did I do that was ever great?
Did I meet the mission?
Did I recognize truth,
or did I think it all fiction?
When trials and tribulations came,
did I faint, or did I come out strong?
Did I remember my faith?
What will You say when I meet You at the gate?
What will You say, God?

On that glorious day,
when the bells ring and the trumpets play,
can I give away my worries?
Can I shed my pains?
Can I truly find peace and rest,
where the sun always shines,
and it never rains?
What will You say, God?

God, I'm just idling wondering,
what will keep us motivated in our other sphere?
Will we skate on an icy lake so clear?
Will we clap, and shout, and cheer

for our favorite ball team,
and rejoice with our peers?
Will we have a family picnic?
Can we bask in the sun?
Can we run in the sand?
Can we fly, oh so high, in the sky?
Where can we find our amusement,
or will we even entertain this movement?
Just wondering, God, what will I do for eternity?
I rest my case in your hands.
I know You have everything worked out perfectly.
What will You say, God?

God, I don't know what heaven is like.
I've been told it's a paradise.
I've been led to believe that I cannot be touched,
I can't be hurt,
and my eyes will not flow with tears of grief.
I can't imagine the joy and peace.
It will be a pleasant relief.
What will You say, God?

And, God, when I see You coming,
am I going to run and hide,
or will I run to You with my arms open wide?
Did I stand up well under circumstances that I could not control,
or did I fall and fold,
and let the devil take the toll?
There is no life without You God,
just an existence;
and who cares to be in that state of retentions?
What will You say, God?

Did I judge others, and think that I was better than them?
What does the Bible say?
Did I try to play God?

That certainly was not my job.
What will You say, God?

And when I leave this old earth,
will I have left it a better place,
or did I just take up space?
Did I forget to give, and just consume?
Did I spread happiness,
or did I spread gloom?
What will You say, God?

Youth, enjoy yourselves.
The world was made for you,
and what I've said is true.
Read Ecclesiastes 11:9,
and many other places, too.
For on your shoulders you
carry the load to maintain the future,
that all may be treated fairly, and not just a few.
What will You say, God?

With all the miracles you have performed,
with all the forces at your command,
please help me,
God, to understand.
With faith and trust, I must abide,
if I expect to make it to the other side.
What will You say, God?

And when I thought all was finished,
You sent me the Red Bird,
my faith to replenish.
How marvelous You are;
You, Jesus, the bright and morning star.
Oh, God, hold my hand wherever You are.
What will You say, God?

Bobbie Lavender

Did I stop to show my gratitude,
or did I take the moment with a greedy attitude?
What can You say of my life, dear God?
Was it well spent; how much do I have to repent?
Oh, dear God, have mercy on my soul.
It's all over, the story has been told.
What will You say, God?

And though my wounds are deep,
and my scars are wide,
I know, in the end,
with You, I will abide.
I am so thankful for Your love.
You will always find me praying with my hands folded,
and pointed towards heaven above.

And when I look up at the sky,
and wonder why;
when I look around
and see all the suffering and pain,
I always cry.
Why is this person, or that person,
mauled and lamed?
Did they not know You?
Did they not call on your name?
Life is so hard and unfair,
then, I remembered, the Lord said,
"I will never give you more than you can bear."
What will You say, God?

Spread the cards.
See what you hold.
Can you use strategy,
do you need to fold,
or do you pass?
One has this, and one has that.

We all have to combat.
And isn't it mystifying how all things work
together to maintain
the existence of life as we know it?
Sometimes the sun shines, sometimes it rains.
What will You say, God?

What is time, and where does it go?
It was here one minute,
and then it was gone.
Sometimes it's fast and sometimes it's slow.
One thing for sure, time will pass;
time will flee.
And, by the way, dear God,
how long is eternity?
And, I hope, as the days grow old,
that your story of glory, will always be told.
What will You say, God?

God, Your ways, I do not understand.
And yet, I try to put everything in your hands.
I do not have the magic plan.
Actually, I have no plan at all.
I am very small.
How do I know what is right or wrong?
I had my chance.
I blew it to the wind,
and now it is all gone.
My only hope is in the mercy of God,
for only He, alone, can atone.
What will You say, God?

Oh, God, when I am tempted,
please give me wisdom,
and guide me through.
Help me, to make my convictions be true.

Bobbie Lavender

I must do what is right.
I cannot, should not, try to plot my own plight.
I do not have the intelligence, nor the insight.
What will You say, God?

This world is my Father's creation.
Why do I worry about suffering and temptation?
I must learn to lean on His arm;
to take all my concerns to the Lord
There, I will be protected from all harm.
My Father promised this;
therefore, there should be no cause for alarm.
All is calm with the LORD.
Rest in peace,
and know that you are loved by God's holy kingdom above.
What will You say, God?

You took my family away, one by one.
The pain was deep, and I was left in despair.
My heart was torn and ripped apart.
Did You see me? Did You care?
Will my life ever be the same?
Who am I to blame?
I know that I should not complain.
You have greater things in store for me.
I'll just have to wait and see.
What will You say, God?

And, when in heaven, there was conflict;
and Lucifer took 30% as his share, that was scary.
Did his followers know the consequence,
or did they even care?
I'm so thankful that I chose to love my Lord,
and follow His plan,
that someday I could come home,
and be in paradise.

The end will come,
and I will have paid the price.
What will You say, God?

Please, dear God, let me know.
I have wondered so.
What path should I take,
what must I endure?
Where do I go?
Do I have anything to show?
I surrender all to God above.
I don't have anything more.
This is the choice I made.
Let the sparks enrage,
and the love and glory never fade.
I love You, God,
and to think of the price you paid.
What will You say, God?

God, I have always wondered,
when on my path to the heavenly gate,
will I walk alone, all by myself,
or will I be guided by the Holy Ghost,
or a band of angels?
Will the path be smooth as silk,
or will it be camouflaged with nails?
Will I grow scared, frail, pale, and faint,
or will I feel secure,
and hear the voices of the saints?
What will You say, God?

What will be in store?
I think this is the age-old question of mankind,
for surely, he doesn't want to remain blind.
However, the Bible clearly states that there
is a time, a place, and a season for all; we can only anticipate.

For now, we will have to wait.
God, help us all.
What will You say, God?

What about the people who have hurt me so?
I can think of four, there might be more.
Forgive, forgive, You say.
I think I turned my problem over to You.
I think I did it without too much delay,
but to love them?
Now that's a whole new horse of a different color.
On this command, I'm really going to have to study,
and review my heart, for I
know deep down, it's going to take a lot of thought,
love, and labor.
What will You say, God?

You can open my windows,
and shut my doors, or visa-versa,
I don't care.
Whichever the choice,
it's going to crush my heart,
and bleed my gut.
Nothing is ever going to be the same,
no matter what.
Wake up!
Your world is not going to be filled with sugar and lace.
There will be many sorrows, trials, and tests, that you will face.
I know that my God will not lead me wrong,
and that I must do my part, and carry on.
What will You say, God?

We'll let God man the ship.
We will be below.
We will row and row.
Isn't that the way it is supposed to go?

With all our efforts,
with all our might,
we will pull and pull to demonstrate our love,
to befriend our friends,
and to shun our foes.
We will take account,
and not go where the devil goes.
What will You say, God?

I did not know yesterday,
what I know today;
nor do I know what's down the road
and around the bend.
Only God knows how it will end.
I cannot predict what rock my foot will touch,
or to what extent the pain will claim.
I just know it's the viper's pit,
and in God I must trust.
What will You say, God?

Do you prepare for the cold winds when they come,
and they will come, or do you just let the winds blow?
Do you not heed the knowledge that you know?
With the talents that you have been given,
you are asked to multiply your provisions.
You are God's helpers here on earth,
to maintain, improve, and preserve. It's not
yours to destroy, but yours to enjoy.
What will You say, God?

Oh Lord, I come before thee on bended knees.
Please hear my plea.
Cover my being with your protection.
May all my actions proclaim your perfection?
May I rejoice in your proclamation of salvation?
May I now come home, no more to roam?
What will You say, God?

Why have I been so complacent?
Did I not know that the winner takes all?
Did I not know the dealer makes the call?
Watch what you ante-up,
you might be compelled to pay-up.
Did I see the storm brewing?
Did I even have a clue?
Did I run for cover?
Did I include You in my rescue?
Was I thankful when the storm was over?
Oh, God, I hope I did. If not, God, please forgive.
What will You say, God?

I've never gone hungry.
I've never missed a meal.
I've never been cold.
I've always had a coat.
I've always had shelter from the elements.
God has supplied my survival needs.
What a display of love He has for me?
What will You say, God?

I'm not totally naive.
I've had the tools to know and perceive.
That's not the question.
The question is: how did I use them,
and from them, what did I receive?
Thank you, God, for all your gifts;
without them, I could not exist.
What will You say, God?

God set the tone.
He did not leave us alone.
He gave us the Bible for knowledge and for guidance,
and now it is up to us to seek and find.
It tells us of our duties,

and gives us an outline of how to live a life divine.
What will You say, God?

And in my youth,
why did I not make worthy use of my leisure time?
Why did I let it pass,
with no reason or rhyme?
Can I go back, and make up for my neglect?
NO, it's time lost, and I cannot replenish.
I can only reflect,
and pray that in the future I never neglect,
and on any chore, I can complete.
That's my wish.
What will You say, God?

And when I look at my dogs, I could cry.
Why did they come to earth to serve not as I?
They have a spirit, and a soul.
I know, because the Bible told me so.
God created them too.
I know He loves them all, not just a few.
And when I get to heaven,
will they be there?
Will they meet me at the gate to run and play?
Will everything be OK?
What will You say, God?

You have kept things from me for my protection.
Oh, thank You for this conception.
You only let me know, when the time was right.
You knew exactly when to light the candle.
You knew when to show me the light.
Oh, God, why do I ask?
I know You know what is best.
I, a mere mortal, could not
handle the knowledge of things to come.
What will You say, God?

I guess You are wondering why I ask so many questions,
and why I have to know?
I don't want to be ignorant and left in the dark.
I have to know my answers true,
so I will know which road to take,
what to do, where to go, and how to grow.
I need Your guidance from above.
I need Your blessings and Your love.
Please hold my hand and help me through.
Give me "the peace that passes understanding."
I promise I will always be true.
I surrender my life to You.
What will You say, God?

God, I have to be honest;
that's just the way I am,
but really, God, I don't understand.
Where did I come from,
why am I living,
and where am I going?
I have not seen heaven,
if so, I cannot recall.
Why did You make man?
Time and time again,
nations have refused to obey Your rules.
Why do You even want us?
And God, really, where am I going?
I have to tell You that I don't know for sure.
All I have is FAITH.
Please forgive my curiosity,
for I am weak and immature.
You can save me—only You.
Please, God, come to my rescue.
What will You say, God?

Something else that puzzles me beyond all belief is:
how does my mind recognize and recall?
How do I forget, and then remember?
What mechanisms are at work?
How do things work together to produce a thought?
There we go again, all about Trust and Faith.
I cannot see my thoughts,
but there is not a question of their existence.
There they are, magic unseen.
What a phenomenal display that I can't explain.
My thoughts are present, and very persistent.
Oh, man, so minute, don't even try to commute,
you just don' t have the ability;
it is for beyond your perceptibility.
Trust and obey is the way.
What will You say, God?

Each has its cycle, and time moves on.
Each generation,
leaving a remnant for the future continuation.
Each doing his part,
that was assigned his lot.
And isn't it fascinating that the Christmas Cactus
knows when it is Christmas, and time to bloom?
And even the birds know when it is time to migrate.
Each little species doing his assignment in life's confinement,
as God had planned in His first commitment.
And isn't it amazing that God made
each little flower with all its unique parts?
He didn't stop there;
He gave each its own different aroma.
How could that be?
It is so amazing to me.
What will You say, God?

Bobbie Lavender

How many four-leaf clovers did I overlook?
How did I escape the obvious put right before me?
To live in an oblivious state, is not what God meant.
To live is to live in a deep consecration
and to partake of God's great creation.
To exist is to remain in a vacuum
of volunteer functions of organs,
almost void of all surroundings.
There is a difference, I do believe.
We must use our minds and conceive.
Each day is a new day; a gift from God.
A chance to be renewed, to contribute, to act, and to learn.
How could you waste a moment that will never return?
Endure to the end.
That's what God said.
No matter the hardship, the pain, or the toil.
God foresaw the need of this,
to refine our Faith and Trust,
and not to succumb to the devils' lust.
What will You say, God?

As I look back, and retract life's journey,
I cannot recall all the moments in full detail.
Everything seems so minute, it's a blur,
it's foggy and misty, but that's OK,
it's fine, for one day I will see in full scope of all the things,
and all life's moments of love, trust and obedience.
They will fit together with no missing pieces,
and above all emotions,
we will obtain charity and hope.
And somewhere, among the singing of the birds,
and the faint ringing of the bells,
I will hear a whisper of a lovely voice saying,
"Come home, little one, no more do you have to cope.
I am here, you will not have any fears.
No longer will you have to wipe away your river of tears."
What will You say, God?

Oh God, I have to turn all things over to You.
I cannot handle them;
I am not equipped.
Thank You for caring for me,
and for loving me so much.
When facing trials and tribulations,
how many times have I thrown my hands up to heaven?
How many times have I asked for Your help?
How many times were You there for me,
and I did not see?
When I am all alone, and fear finds me nigh,
what does the Bible say?
The scriptures, I cannot deny.
What will You say, God?

Am I covered with fifth and slime?
NO, tell me I am not.
The thought is so repulsive,
and yet the devil slides among the inhabitants of the Earth,
seeking with all his might,
to conquer a soul to include in his clan.
Oh, how happy it makes his claim
to gather together God's precious children for his flock.
What a horrendous crime!
It truly makes my heart pine.
What will You say, God?

God, remember that game we used to play as children,
"Hide and Go Seek?"
We would all hide,
and the person chosen to be "IT,"
would say, "Here I come, ready or not.
"Well, I know that life is not a game,
and You will truly be ready, with arms open wide,
to welcome us all home.
Yet, as I look back,

not one of us were ever lost.
We all were found, or made it back home.
"Allie, Allie all in free," we would say.
And at bedtime, we were all present,
and accounted for, said our prayers,
and were called by name.
For all of us, I know in my heart,
You will do the same.
What will You say, God?

Hello Jesus. Is that You at the door?
Come on in, You're so welcome.
And in my house,
will You recognize the pictures in the frames?
How could You not know that loving face,
that kind smile?
And look again,
You will find the Good Book,
the Holy Bible, in each room, ready to be read.
You can see, I have no pornography.
I engage in religious thoughts and deeds.
I am a follower, and a Christian.
It has been my pride.
And, how many times, incognito,
have You been my guest, and I was unaware?
Did I gather, did I arrive?
Touch me.
You will see.
The Holy Ghost encompasses my aura.
It is engraved in stone; it cannot flee.
The Holy Ghost will always be with me.
What will You say, God?

In void of the working mechanisms of the universe,
of course, I wonder HOW,
of course, I wonder WHY.

I don't know how these phenomena engage in synchronizations.
One day is gone, another day moves in.
I guess this is the way it's always been.
How do I live in all this commotion?
Do I give, and expect compensation?
Lord, please let my life be simple.
Please Lord, let my life be an example.
What will You say, God?

I don't remember asking for this fight.
Some say I did;
some say I didn't.
Why should I wonder
if it's too late to even ponder?
And who do I think that I am,
to even question God's plan?
I'm just a little speck.
You would hardly notice.
I'm camouflaged, mauled, and shredded.
I'm disfigured beyond recognition.
I am a complete wreck.
You say there is hope for me.
Oh, what love must abide in You,
Jesus, to save a soul such as mine.
Oh, God, I've made a mess.
Can things ever be put back, right?
And on the darkest night,
let me see the brilliant light.
What will You say, God?

Oh, God, don't let me be an offender of pain and suffering.
Let me be a mender.
I don't prefer to mingle among the bad and disrespectful.
I much desire to circulate among the kind, loving, and beautiful
Am I going to see the Pearly Gates?
Am I going to walk the Golden Streets?

Bobbie Lavender

I just can't imagine.
I can't realize.
What it is all about?
I pray that I stood true,
and on my beliefs,
I didn't once compromise.
I hope in all my choices,
with Your guidance, I was always wise.
What will You say, God?

On a certain occasion, not once,
but trice I was tempted.
I triumphantly won the banner of glory.
I resisted temptations with a strong heart and a fortress will,
with God holding my hand.
My character has proven to meet the challenge.
May the devil rest in hell,
that deceitful, lying, contrite evil creature.
Who does he think he is that he could reign and play God?
May he be struck dead with a blazing red hot rod.
When this world grows so weird,
like "when a snake grows a beard,"
may the devil be crushed, shredded, torn apart, made to bleed,
(oh, he doesn't have blood).
Oh, stop. Yours is not to rule and control.
You are not to say, "when, how, what and why."
You are not to go there. You don't dare.
I don't know the things that I must bear,
but I do know that things will be OK,
if You are there.
My God my Father, I concede, I bow.
What will You say, God?

It's all in God's time to choose and pick.
He is all powerful, and He knows in a moment,
He is so quick, but let me say,

I know in my heart that He is love divine,
and He will be fair.
I know that I will be His,
and shine in glory; this I can surely declare.
Be still, my soul.
Let Jesus, my sins behold,
and terminate evil,
and bring peace to this world.
I know it can appear;
I have been told.
What will You say, God?

Sometimes, I feel like I live in limbo.
I don't know which way to turn, what to do,
or where to go. I must rely on You, dear God.
When tragedy strikes, and it will,
even on the healthy and the wealthy, please,
dear God, give us the strength,
help us all to bear the trials,
and keep us safe and healthy.
When times get rough,
I remember FROG (Forever Rely On Jesus).
And, when You come to visit me,
that is why You will see the Bible,
pictures of God, and lots and lots of FROGS.
What will You say, God?

Sometimes, you are compelled
to get it right on the first chance;
if not, the moment will flee,
and all efforts will become history.
Be ready, be fortified, for in the end,
it is God you need to glorify.
Oh, God, I bow my head in reverence to become humble.
I pray that I have not caused division,
but have brought forth unification.

Bobbie Lavender

Have I spent my life offending?
I hope, rather, I have spent it giving.
What will You say, God?

We come for a little while;
we don't stay long,
and then in a short time,
we are gone.
Did I do what I could,
while I could,
or was I oblivious and let all the others
run while I stood?
Oh, God, I hope I did my part.
I hope I let my light shine,
and I hope I always chose
to depart from the dark.
For evil is hideous.
It destroys, and brings turmoil.
It is God's wish that is rightness,
and goodness will rise,
and prevail for all.
God is love.
He loves with a depth which is immeasurable,
and far outreached in our vision.
What will You say, God?

I am a free performing agent,
not a puppet or a technical machine.
I make my choices; I choose and pick.
Within a split second,
I must decide what is right and what is wrong.
Am I that quick?
Did I use this power with integrity,
or did I think it was my glory?
Yes, it is so true, just think about it.
"Only God can make a tree."

All the power to God Almighty.
I humbly dedicate my life unto Thee.
What will You say, God?

Why did I get old and crippled?
Why could I have not stayed young and spry?
Did I know that I was going to die?
Yes, but not incapacitated.
I wanted to run to heaven,
and not walk on a cane,
and certainly not in all this pain.
Why do I question?
You have the answers,
You have the master plan.
Your ways are not my ways,
I do not understand. Forgive me,
God, for one day I will see the light,
and only then,
I will know that everything is going to be alright.
What will You say, God?

Do You really care, God?
I saved a little bird's life today.
After he recuperated,
he flew away.
Do You really care?
I helped a little child,
I opened a door for an elderly man,
I said my prayers and phrased
Your name.
All this, I performed in solitude,
without any fame.
Did You see?
Did You hear?
Do You really care?
What will You say, God?

Where are all the pieces to the puzzle?
Why can't I make them fit?
Why is there always a gap?
A space that is always open,
and not complete?
God, are You going to fix everything?
Is everything going to be OK?
Should I worry, or fret, that I might get lost,
and never be found in all this decay?
What will You say, God?

Oh, God, where are You?
Where are You?
Are You far, or near?
Did You speak?
Why can I not hear?
I need Your help.
I cannot carry my weight,
I cannot comply.
I can only feel NOW.
I have not lived in "What's to come."
Oh, God help me to conform.
Bring me safely home.
What will You say, God?

Grief is a terrible thing.
It reached into my heart, and tore it apart.
Why did my love ones have to go?
Why did it have to be so?
Oh, I know,
I know it was in Your master plan long, long ago.
What will You say, God?

This hurt passed through my heart
 and went right to my soul.
It took my warmth away,

and knocked me out cold.
What do I do now?
I don't know if I should hold on, or fold.
I don't know. What should I do?
I can't foretell.
Do I lie down and die,
or do I fight like hell?
What will You say, God?

Sometimes, it is difficult to distinguish
between right and wrong,
but I do diligently try to clarify.
In my heart,
I sincerely desire to do thy will,
of this, I cannot deny.
And, God, why did I make so many mistakes?
What was I looking for?
Was it love, or security, or just my place?
Why did I not slow down,
and seek Your will, but no,
I did not, and now I must pay the bill.
Do not forsake me, dear Lord.
What will You say, God?

What did I do so wrong?
I know that I am weak, and not very strong.
I know that in the end,
we will all be gone;
but that is so far in the future,
that's for another era, another new morning,
at the break of dawn.
What will You say, God?

What is that old saying, how does it go?
"You don't miss the water until the well goes dry."
"You don't miss the lights until the electricity goes out

"Just compare the things we take for granted.
Life is made more comfortable with modern inventions,
yet, these very things have added to the complexity of life.
How do we cope?
How do we strive?
Can we encompass, maintain, and stay alive?
What will You say, God?

And for my acts of generosity,
I would be a fool to expect to receive compensation.
If I have one ounce of regret,
it would be better to keep what I have, and of giving, forget.
Forget what I have done,
and concentrate on what's to come.
What will You say, God?

I'm not so smart, but yet,
I know, I have been given so much.
God, on me,
You did abundantly give a million gifts,
and blessings, of which I consider my lack of worthiness.
I cannot repay.
I don't even try.
It's true, I accept,
but I always say, "Thank You."
Let me reiterate.
I cannot thank You enough,
and like the ten leopards You healed,
and only one turned back to express his gratitude.
On, God, let me be the one.
What will You say, God?

Oh God, when so many years have come and gone
and I no longer can steady my balance;
I am weak, not strong.
Do not forsake me.

Let me walk with steady feet as You guide the way,
and cast away my fears,
and take away my tears.
Lead me, guide me, show me the way.
I will follow, humbly, gratefully, all in admiration.
There will be no delay.
I come to You today.
What will You say, God?

The journey has been long,
the wide road, bumpy, but through the barriers,
and the roadblocks,
You could see ahead.
I followed, and You lead.
As I reminisce,
I just wish I had more to give,
to present before my Lord,
my Prince.
What will You say, God?

For You, Dear Lord,
have I been an ambassador of goodwill?
There is so much to do.
Let me jump in.
Let me get my hands dirty in an effort to help others,
because, I too have been so blessed.
Come, let's all rally.
Let's keep our focus on the mission cause,
and reap what's in it for us.
Be ready for action when you hear the SOS.
Jump right in, don't be shy.
Rally up to the rescue.
It's all up to you.
How will you reply?
What will You say, God?

And when You see me walking down the street,
know for sure that I have tasted the bitter and the sweet.
I must confess, that sweet is better than bitter.
Between the two, there is absolutely no contest.
My life, God,
I put in Your hands;
let me rest.
Try to always seek the sweet,
for bitter is to defeat.
What will You say, God?

I saw a little deer today,
killed on the side of the road.
It was so young, that it had not lost its spots
God, You take some very young,
some somewhere in between,
and some very old.
We are not told.
We only see part of the vast picture.
We are instructed to live in faith, love, trust, obedience,
and to endure to the end.
We shall see Your mighty master plan one day,
and then we will understand.
Oh, God, hold us in Your loving arms.
Protect us from gloom, evil and harm.
Help us to keep Your commandments,
bring us safely home, where we belong.
Let us see that magnificent heaven,
where love abounds,
where we hear the little birds sing and all glory shines,
where no tears are shed, and nothing goes wrong.
What will You say, God?

Please hear me,
God, a weak and mortal creature that I am.
I know that things are planned,

and all is not just incidental.
As each day unfolds,
what blessings will I behold?
Will I follow the rules of the good book,
or will I disregard what I have been told?
I need Your love. I was never meant to be alone.
God, have mercy on my soul.
Maintain my gait,
I cannot make it on my own.
What will You say, God?

Be still my heart,
and listen, for when you are talking,
you cannot hear.
Everything has its limitation,
and of that, I am no exception.
Was I always aloof,
or was I searching for the truth?
Was I aware of what
followed me, or waited for me in the lair?
Oh, God, don't give me more than I can bear,
for I know it is You, and only You,
that knows my heart's despair.
What will You say, God?

Everything is in perfect harmony.
When the moment arrives,
act instantly, without hesitation.
The moment is golden.
To waste it would be a sin,
and I have acquired enough of them.
What will You say, God?
And when the lightning struck,
and the thunder roared, and water covered my face,
I knew the fight was commencing.
I remembered that I could swim,

I could float,
and I knew what the Bible wrote.
I knew for sure that this would pass.
The sun always shines, gloom would not last.
What will You say, God?

Oh, God. no one has the right to judge,
or criticize me in my love for You.
Have mercy on me.
I will stand before You on that great day in awe.
My life will be in full view,
You always knew what I would do.
I will no longer be pestered with the devil.
His crew will be left behind.
I can't remember him being invited to the party.
This is just between God and me,
of what was, and what will be.
What will You say, God?

Please help me forget the "Ifs" in life.
"What if ?"
What if I had chosen different avenues along life's path,
what should it have been,
could it have been,
what would it have been?
Let me live the course that has been allocated to me.
Let me strive to conquer, defeat,
and accomplish the goal for ever situation
that confronts me along life's way.
To accomplish anything,
I am fully aware that I need You walking by my side.
On my own, I can accomplish nothing.
I know that in You, I must always confide.
Help me, God, be my guide.
What will You say, God?

Are You going to come back like You said You would?
Are You going to make everything
new like You said You could?
How long do I wait?
How long will it take?
"Endure to the end," that is what You said.
I plow through this wildness,
trying to do the best that I can.
I try to have faith in that which I cannot see.
I try to have hope in what tomorrow will bring.
Make me strong for tomorrow's encounters.
May my fruits be received with acknowledgements of true love.
I wait now, patiently,
for Your word sent from above.
Be with me, hold my hand,
then I will know that everything will be OK,
everything will be just grand.
What will You say, God?

Your promises are true.
You cannot tell a lie,
so why do some things I deny?
Why do I not see the truth,
and on You totally rely?
And when things got tough,
and I through I could take no more,
did I want to go on,
or did I seek strength from heaven above?
Did I realize what You shed for me;
did I realize Your love?
What will You say, God?

Holy, Holy is Your Word.
Did I believe this with all my heart and might?
Did I catch onto the rope;
did I hold it tight?
What will You say, God?

With the Bible as my guide,
and the commandants to follow,
did I put forth the faith to form my way?
Did I become the best that I could be,
and always willing, my debt to pay?
What will You say, God?

Did I trust, or did I doubt?
What is life all about?
Did I forgive, so that I might be forgiven?
Did I see others as my sisters and brothers?
Will I be different,
or will I be indifferent,
like so many others?
Did I go second,
that others might go first,
or was I inconsiderate and did not bother
with the feelings of my sisters and brothers?
What will You say, God?

Oh, God, hear my plea.
Do not forsake us.
Do not leave us to wonder on our own.
Hold our hands.
Lead the way.
We will follow, we will obey
What will You say, God?

We come for a little while;
we don't stay long,
and then in a short time,
we are gone!
Did I do what I could,
while I could, or was I oblivious,
and let all the others run
while I stood?

Oh, God, I hope that I did my part.
I hope that I let my light shine,
and I hope that I always chose to depart from the dark.
For evil is hideous, it destroys, and brings turmoil;
it brings pain, suffering and devastation.
It is God's wish that rightness
and goodness will rise and prevail for all.
God is love, with a depth which is immeasurable,
and for outreached from our minute ability to understand.
What will You say, God?

Remember the day I said,
"I'm tuff, I can take it?"
I'm wondering now, can I retract?
I'm not as strong as I proclaimed.
I need Your love;
I need Your care.
I find myself hurting
and lamed.
I really need to call on Your name.
What will You say, God?

And on my journey to heaven,
as I walk the path,
will someone be with me,
or do I tread alone?
I need Your presents;
I need Your love.
And to my heart so close,
here are some things You wrote:
The ten commandments.
You are the Alpha and the Omega
All Your promises of love and support
The Beatitudes
The Bible-
a guide for our lives that we might learn

from the past, and take a peek into the future.
You taught us the way of life.
Jesus gave His life that we might live.
Your acts were without hesitations...not reservations!
I have no force to install without Your will.
I do have limits and boundaries of restrain,
which I do not understand.
What will You say, God?

You gave us Your love.
You gave us Your all from above.
You showed us how to live in love,
and how to peacefully congregate.
You also told us of the things that You hate:
there are six; make it one more,
and that will be seven.
Haughty eyes
A lying tongue
Hands that shed innocent blood.
A heart that devises wicked plans.
Feet that run to evil.
False witness.
One who sows discord among his clan.
What will You say, God?

How many times did You save my life,
and I didn't even know?
How many times have You called my name,
and I did not reply?
How many times did You prepare my way,
and I rebelled, and didn't even try?
How many times does it take before there is no more?
How many times, dear Lord, do You repeat?
How many times before it is too late?
How many times, dear Lord,
do we get a second chance?

How many times, before we meet You at the gate?
How many times, dear Lord, does it take?
What will You say, God?

Oh, God, I intensely feel,
I humbly kneel.
To You, I earnestly appeal,
just hold my hand as I walk and pray.
Did I shine brightly,
As a star, or was I engulfed with disgrace?
Will I be lost or found?
Will I wear a starry crown?
Did I do things right?
What will be my plight?
What will You say, God?

What did I gain?
Was it worth the pain?
What made me so thoughtless?
What made me so vain,
When all I wanted was to hear Your name?
Will my life ever be the same?
Will I always be weak and lame,
or will I find justice and fame?
What will You say, God?

Did I flutter about in airy society,
or did I look for a solid foothold in a basic foundation?
Was I even thinking about Your sacrifice and salvation?
Did I think about my future,
or did I just want instant gratification?
What will You say, God?

Did I ask to come down here?
Did I ask to stay?
What must I pay?

Will my scars and sins of life be washed away?
Can I once again run free and play?
What Will You say, God?

Will I be a prisoner,
or will I be free?
Can I make a deal when the time arrives,
or am I compelled to pay the fee?
What will it be?
What will You say, God?

Where were You, God,
when I needed You so?
Were You by my side,
and I didn't know?
Did You look into my eyes,
and I did not see that You will always be near,
and help me?
What will You say, God?

I try to see the light at the end of the tunnel,
but it is not very bright:
in fact, sometimes it is completely out of sight.
Sometimes, I don't think life is worth the fight.
I don't always know what is wrong or right.
I try and I try with all my might,
but when I look back, what do I see?
I see just a lot of time lost and misery.
All is doomed, all is vanity.
Only God can save my sanity.
What will You say, God?

Just look around.
God's greatness is magnified.
It surrounds the universe.
It is the story of the gospel for all,

it's the message we all must discuss.
We listen, we learn, and then we must choose.
Choose wisely, child of God,
or you will certainly lose.
What will You say, God?

It's not all about me.
It's about my friends and family.
What touches one, touches all.
We need to be considerate of the big and the small.
We are all in this together,
throughout the entire world.
It is the way God planned it, come what may.
If it is God's will, I will obey.
Oh, God, before thee, I bow, I pray.
What will You say, God?

Don't let the moment take you on a flying space trip.
The moment will end, the trip will stop,
and where will you be?
Will you be proud of yourself, or longing to retreat?
Will you desire a big eraser
to eradicate all your mistakes,
or will you turn your back and flee?
Oh, the choices we do make;
all within the blink of the eye,
and without a second to debate!
Watch what you say, what you do,
and with whom you congregate;
it will all come back to you late in the evening.
Sometimes we know,
other times it has no meaning.
What will You say, God?

There are some things that money won't buy...
happiness, love, or a quilt free heart.

Some things carry a mark that is impossible to eradicate.
They are perfectly embedded below the skin.
You put them there,
and when you are so careless in your taste,
how do you expect to win?
Oh, God, what does the future behold?
That's the ultimate question that mortals seek,
but if we knew, we would not need faith.
So, what chance do I have?
Take it to the Lord.
What will You say, God?

What was that?
Was it the flutter of an angel's wing,
or the chimes of a bell?
No, I do believe it was the full grown sound
of the trumpet's blast.
Dear Jesus, when will You come again?
I know You will descend on a cloud so clear,
and the trumpet's shrill will announce Your presence.
I'll hear my name called;
I'll see the saints.
Oh, what a glorious occasion.
Oh, what a commotion.
Will it be too much for me to visualize?
Will I be composed through all the fanfare,
or will I grow weak and faint?
I must not, I know that I can't.
Turn a page in the Book of Life,
and let me see.
I want to be ready when You are ready for me.
What will You say, God?

It is stated that all the knowledge we on earth obtain
will be granted us in heaven to retain.
It clearly states that the knowledge

we now know will be to our advantage.
I did my best, and studied diligently,
but there were a billion things to learn;
with this you must agree.
I could never conceive
how a 575 tons plane could glide so easily in the sky,
or the identity of a male or female crawfish.
I don't know, and I could never learn the anatomy of a snail,
or why it moves so slowly.
I have always wondered how things work.
I want to know the minute details of the mechanism.
I have put forth much effort in my search,
and I could never comprehend the miracle of my birth.
What will You say, God?

When I see You face to face,
and when You hold me in Your arms,
I will still wonder....
What will You say, God?

And, Oh God, before I go,
may I proclaim the many thanks
for Your gifts from above?
Thank You for the air I breathe.
Thank You for the food I eat.
Thank You for the clothes I wear.
Thank You for the water I drink.
Thank You for the sights I see.
Thank You for the sounds I hear.
Thank You for the touch I feel.
Thank You for my shelter that protects me from the elements.
Thank You for the bed where I sleep,
to keep me secure and provide me rest.
Oh, God, I am blessed.
What will You say, God?

How was I so blind, when I came to earth?
Why could I not predict what I would be?
Why could I not see?
What would it take to awaken me?
When I was young and spry, and in my youth,
I never thought I would shrivel up and die.
The Bible says so in the end,
and we must "Endure to the end.
"What will You say, God?

Now, what was that number on the gate?
Do I just walk in, or do I wait?
Do I wait in line for my name to be heard,
or do I rush in front of others to take my turn?
What do I do? Oh, woe is me.
I have no clue.
Oh, let me retract.
I think I knew, I just refused to enter my plea.
Oh, woe is me.
What will You say, God?

In this world of so many angles,
I feel like a pea washed out to sea.
Where is my place?
Where can it be?
Oh, God, give me security.
Give me strength to weather this storm,
and a heart to conform.
Help me meet my foe with full capacity.
This will be my plea.
Will You help me?
What will You say, God?

Oh, what do You do with a person like me,
who knows, but wants to play ignorant?
And what do You do with the people who are ignorant,

but want others to think they are smart?
What confusion, what 's the conclusion?
And what do You do with people who balk;
that don't know the difference between sugar and salt?
How do You contend with us day in and day out?
How do You love us so?
Of course, read the Bible,
Your Holy Word,
to find the answers, and be in the know.
What will You say, God?

When You come again,
and You promised to,
will You govern with peace and security?
Will we have any hopes of prosperity?
Will we live with joy and happiness?
Will we have, for all mankind,
a joyful attitude, and be able to express our gratitude?
I surely hope so.
It will be my destination,
then I can truly understand your intended constitution.
What will You say, God?

And, God, there's something I must ask:
with all the talents that You have disposed,
why can't people help without monetary pay?
Why must we be forced to reach into our purse?
Is it a blessing or a curse?
I surely hope when the occasion occurs,
that I volunteer, and serve in Your name,
and do not expect money for my fame.
I hope that I am good and pure,
and love You so.
I hope that all my pursuits are a blessing for You,
and that of me,
You are never ashamed.

Bobbie Lavender

Oh, God, I praise Your name.
What will You say, God?

When I made my choice,
and was deeply involved in my pursuit,
did I stop and face the fact that it was done?
It could not be erased.
My action was over.
It was complete.
I did not have a second chance.
It was written in stone.
It was written in the Book of Life.
It was a fact.
It was my fate.
Let me not reiterate,
nor contemplate of " what was,"
or "what will be,"
but let me be of a cheery countenance,
so others might see in me a bright shiny light.
Then I will know that everything is going to be alright
I hope I haven't been stubborn nor contentious.
I am Your child,
and that's what makes it worthwhile .
What will You say, God?

There are two roads in life:
the Thorny Hill Road
and the Rose Garden Road.
Why did I choose the Thorny Hill Road?
Aw----, it looked like so much fun.
The streets were filled with gayety.
Why not join in, and take my turn?
Little did I know those beautiful shiny thorns
would cut, maul, and destroy my soul.
I have the scars, cuts, and bruises to prove
what I chose not to control.

Only God knows what will be foretold.
How low can you go before God will pull you from below?
I asked His help to be pulled
from the twisted and confined vines of the sharp thorns.
Only God can open the doors,
and save me from the treacherous storms.
Only God can wash me clean.
Only God knows what is unseen.
I come before You on bended knees.
Hear my plea,
I pray Oh God,
have mercy on me, please.
What will You say, God?

"If you don't use it, you will lose it,"
and soon, you don't even miss it.
Love is so fragile.
It comes from your soul,
at the bottom of your heart.
Treat it well.
Nurture it deeply,
or soon it will depart.
So little, so late,
what difference does it make?
Oh God, let me be the one
who helps those in need,
and never, never be so vain as to count my deeds.
Love, life, and death;
the things in life that we must face.
God help us as we run the race.
What will You say, God?

When I picked up that coral snake,
how did I know that death was only 30 seconds away?
How many times have You saved me,
and watched over me night and day?

Bobbie Lavender

How could I imagine the pain
that I would endure when
You called my son, my little child back home to You?
I don't know, I can't compare.
Oh God, how many times have You seen me through?
How did I know that cancer had invaded my body,
and endangered my life?
asked You to hold my hand,
and I saw peace.
How many times did I flirt with death?
How many times did You command the threat to cease?
What will You say, God?

Did I run and hide,
so I wouldn't have to abide?
I don't know, but I do know that I must face the day,
come what may
What will You say, God?

When all the fun was taken out of my life,
I thought all things were not worth the fight.
Even though I tried, with all my might,
I just could not see the future;
there, for me, wasn't any light.
With all the strength that remained in my body,
I tried one more time to pull through.
I remembered You said,
"I will always be with you."
What will You say, God?

Do You call us home one by one?
Do You know when
we will take our last breath here on earth,
and our first breath behind the veil?
How do the ones left behind prevail?
Why do some go fast, and others linger on?

Why do some suffer pain,
and others don't have to complain?
Why do some go early,
and are denied the full cycle of life?
There will always be the scar;
I pray not the open wound.
When will You come, Jesus, how soon?
Be with the broken hearted, wipe away the grief.
Oh, God, our life here is so brief.
What will You say, God?

Don't exactly know where I came from;
don't exactly know where I am going.
suppose you might say that I am lost.
Only God can lead me on the path
that I must take, and I must take
each step in the blindness of faith.
This I must do at all costs.
What is my reward?
I'm not exactly sure,
but I do know that I must endure.
Faith, love, and hope;
I must set these as my priorities.
I must remember at all times,
and through all trials,
that God is my Father,
He is the ultimate authority.
I know that my God loves me.
What will You say, God?

When things don't turn out in life like they should,
from your view.
You can rank, rave, cuss, and fuss all you want.
It does not change the course; it only makes it worst.
What will You say, God?

I have to live with what I do.
Give me the strength to change for the good,
and endure.
I am responsible for what I do.
I am responsible for what I see.
I am responsible for what I think.
I am responsible for all my actions.
Help me to build a character fortified with armor against all evil.
This is my desire; this is my prayer.
Please help me to always be aware.
What will You say, God?

You must be on guard.
You must be aware,
for you can never anticipate
when the devil will rise and strike.
He can appear as quickly as a storm, or gale,
and he will delight to harm you with his forked tail.
He's been known to kill,
and never look back.
He has ruined many a life with his venomous attack.
Oh, God, protect us, keep us in line.
We want to be Yours good and kind.
Protect us from the devil and his host.
He is such an ungodly rebel.
What will You say, God?

"It is what it is."
That is what some say,
but that eradicates faith, hope, and charity.
I'm not sure of that philosophy.
What will You say, God?

Of all the cards that I have been dealt,
and all the pain that I have felt,
wouldn't you think by

now that I would know how to handle the day?
Sometimes it's my thoughts that get in the way,
although, I do pray and pray.
What will You say, God?

I am compelled to fight each day,
just to live, and it shouldn't be that way.
I need to turn to You, dear God,
to show me the path to choose.
I must take the right road,
or I will most surely lose.
I put my life in Your hands,
for I know that You have the master plan.
Help me to do my part.
Help me to complete my mission.
I came to serve, not for glory or recognition,
but for Your phrases and exceptions.
What will You say, God?

I am so truly thankful for God's omnipotence.
He has seen me through stupid endeavors,
and forgiven me of my many mistakes.
How could I have not seen in the moment,
that danger lay ahead, and all for the sake of FUN,
I made myself a very hard bed.
What will You say, God?

I resolved to be a servant of God,
and I am so happy to be.
I rose above the scuff.
I have camouflaged the cuts;
they say I am tough.
It takes a lot of living to live.
God has given me the strength.
Now, I must entrust all that I possess,
and return to God my tenth.

What will You say, God?

Hello God, it's I again,
pulling on Your robe strings.
I'm on my knees asking for things that I think that I need.
I just don't know what to say when I pray.
It is well and good that You know my every concern.
You know my necessaries before I ask.
What will You say, God?

How well You keep Your garden, God.
No flower knows when it is going to rain,
yet, they sparkle in all their glory
exhibiting Your creation of magnificence.
Their beauty so shines, as an exhibition of Your omnificence.
I, too, must be a flower in Your garden so divine.
What will You say, God?

God's promises are greater than all my fears.
I know that He loves and cares for me.
The Bible tells me so,
and one day He will welcome me home.
He will take away all my sorrows,
and wipe away all my tears.
I will wait.
What will You say, God?

Oh, God, how do You intimately know each of us;
a trillion, plus or more, and not one exactly alike,
yet similar?
What mind boggling mysteries of Your creation.
How do You know where we are,
where we are going, and where we have been?
How many universes do You have?
What number could it be?
What will You say, God?

I can't imagine heaven and the spirit world that awaits me.
What a glorious homecoming that will be,
to be united with You, my family, friends, and pets;
all that I have ever known and as You requested,
I will try to endure to the end.
What will You say, God?

God knows all the answers to the mysteries of life,
and I can only wonder how and why.
I walk blindly through a dark alley
knowing that God is holding my hand.
I cannot see, only faith prevails.
I am blinded by darkness now,
but somewhere in the near future,
I will be blinded by the bright radiance
of the luminous Morning Star.
In that land, not so far away,
we will all live together in love and harmony.
Your WORD is our guarantee for a heavenly home,
where glory shines all around.
I cannot imagine Your master plan.
Until then, be by my side, hold my hand.
I shall arrive victoriously.
What will You say, God?

I want nothing that does not belong to me.
That is why I am so grateful to give my tenth.
I do it with pleasure and honor, to set before my King.
There is never a delay for that special day.
It fills my heart with glee.
There is nothing here that is really free.
We must all work and strive to meet our goals.
We must be diligent in what we seek.
With the help of God,
may we accomplish our expectations.
May we enjoy a productive good life while we are here?

May we learn our lessons,
without much sorrow and complications?
May we hear, "My good and faithful servant"
when we reach our final destination.
What will You say, God?

I don't know what happened.
I don't know what to do.
Just hold my hand and see me through.
What credits can I declare?
Will my slate be full or bare?
I had my chance.
Why did I not realize what was at stake?
And, when I promenade among the best,
will I be first, second, third, or last,
or will I even be in that number to reminisce about my past?
What will You say, God?

When that call comes,
and tragedy strikes,
when your heart races,
and you feel faint, take time,
call God's name.
He is there for us to calm our pain.
On our spinning planet,
nothing remains the same.
It is in a perpetual state of change.
We face constant challenges,
problems to solve,
and look for strength in which to cope.
What promotes us to barge forward?
It is courage, endurance, faith, and hope.
Yes, nothing remains the same.
It changes from day to day,
and now we must live a different life;
we must walk a different path

as we stumble along our way.
There is only one answer,
and you know.
You must follow Him,
if you expect your life to ever glow.
What will You say, God?

Do I have a right to propose all these questions?
Is it right or wrong,
and why so many, and why so long?
I hope I did not cause despair.
Is it lack of faith,
or is it something I can't contemplate, or compare?
What will You say, God?

Can I brave the storm,
whatever might be?
Do I have a connection?
Can I perform the task with perfection?
Is glory my destination,
and will I always have You as my salvation?
You gave me breath.
We give and take,
and I will always be thankful for Your love,
my family, and the friends I make.
What will You say, God?

Oh, God, please take care of me,
for I am weak and fragile, and easy to break.
Yes, Lord, I have made many mistakes.
The consequences have caused many pains,
and my heart does ache.
Forgive me of that which I should not have partaken.
Renew my life. Let my soul be awakened.
What will You say, God?

I came, I saw, but did I conquer?
I must be strong; I must hold on.
I must meet defeat. I must gain my reward.
And, when I come to Your throne,
I will surrender all. I will kneel at Your feet.
The songs of the angels will be so angelically sweet.
What will You say, God?

Tell me, how did I do?
What was my score?
Was it high or low?
Do I need to do some more?
Why do I always need a sign?
Why can't I be satisfied?
Why can't I live on trust and faith?
Why can't I just live on Your love so divine?
What will You say, God?

I've read of a heaven, and of a hell.
Why, now, do I look so pale?
Could I not distinguish between fantasy and reality?
Why did I not pay attention?
Can I go back and make rectifications?
Can I go back and wipe the slate clean?
I know the answer is NO.
You, dear God, are the only one who can redeem.
What will You say, God?

I am only a lowly creature, put here on this planet to roam.
This is not my permanent home.
My mission is to prepare for my heavenly mansion.
I do not have time to squander, and waste my commission.
God is watching me, and my actions.
I must be careful in what I pursue.
I must be ready for the rescue.
It will come in a blink of the eye;

like a thief in the night.
Oh, God, here am I.
Please don't pass me by.
What will You say, God?

I don't have the words to elaborate.
I don't have the strength to fight off the devil's bait.
You are all that I have, God.
Come to my rescue. Save me by my faith.
I know that You want us to live in perfect harmony.
Where did we miss the mark?
Why are things so dark?
Let the light shine through,
and I will know that all is true.
Let us be submissive.
Let us be obedient.
Our rewards will be far beyond our imagination.
Let us all gain salvation.
What will You say, God?

Why didn't I look in the good book,
or did I even know where to look?
Will I find mercy at Your feet
or will I be declined?
What will I face?
Will I like my new place?
What will You say, God?

For all the evil and scary people,
who came to Earth to prey,
do You have a special place for them to stay?
Am I compelled to be with them, side by side?
Do I have to fight them, do I have to abide,
or can I find peace, and run and hide?
Will You gather me in Your arms,
and protect me from all harm?

Oh, God, will I have a second chance?
Will You wash me whiter than snow?
Will my soul be all aglow?
What will You say, God?

As I look back,
would I have changed my lot?
Was it a bad attitude?
Was I strong?
Did I have a strong fortitude?
Surely, I would like to have polished my route.
It would have made life so much better.
Yes, I would have changed a lot.
They will just put me in the ground to rot.
God, I don't understand Your rules.
I have read and studied diligently,
but there are so many things I forgot.
What will You say, God?

How do You deal with me,
when I have been so asinine?
Why did I not see what was so obvious?
How did things go by?
Why did I not try to catch them?
They flew by so fast,
and now I lie in my bed and cry.
What will You say, God?

Now, that you are out in this world,
and on your own,
don't forget the things we talked about.
Hold on tightly, with all your might.
If you live by God's Word,
EVERYTHING WILL BE ALRIGHT.
What will You say, God?

What is life all about?
Is it a dream, or is it reality?
Is it something like the little bird that flew in from somewhere,
landed on a branch,
stayed a short while,
and then flew away?
Where did he go?
I cannot say. I
do not have a crystal ball to foretell,
and predict the future's call.
I am in the hands of God;
He is in control.
Some things I need to know;
some things are yet to be told.
God has promised we will someday
be enlightened of all His ways.
The complete story will be revealed at His chosen time;
on His timeline,
not mine.
What will You say, God?

The sun will shine someday,
even, if just for a while,
and in my heart,
I know that I must smile,
and go that extra mile.
I don't have an earthly eternity.
I just have a little while.
What was that number?
Do I have it in my files?
Can I call on heaven above
to issue me comfort, and love?
Where I came from,
I'm not quite sure,
and where I'm going is out of sight.
All I know is right NOW,

and NOW is a moment;
it's gone in a blink,
and quickly becomes yesterday's history,
written in ink.
What will You say, God?

Don't tell me that we are so shallow,
and spoiled, and immature,
that we think things appear
without blood, sweat, and tears.
When will we realize
that things come with a price?
Someone must spend the time, and sacrifice.
God, forgive me for asking why.
I just wanted to know. I am so inquisitive.
I can't wait. I have to know my fate.
Oh, yes, I know what the Bible says,
and I know that I must wait.
I will see clearly then, face to face.
I will see the view, from angles unnumbered
and know that with God,
all things are true.
I must endure.
What will You say, God?

Was I strong and staunch,
and set in my ways;
determined to proclaim
the gospel for others to seek knowledge,
and expect salvation?
Did I follow after Jesus,
and teach the Good News?
How many people's lives did I touch?
I hope that I left a mark for others to seek,
and I pray that I was strong for the sake of others,
and certainly, not weak.

We only have a short time in which to prove our worth.
God loves all His children, and in return,
we must all strive
to do our best to show respect, and love.
God showed His love for us,
when He sent Jesus to earth.
What will You say, God?

What can I do to make this a better place?
I do not want to be idle, and take up space.
I was put here to prove my love for You.
It was my job, my duty to do.
Will I be chosen, will I be one of the few?
I hope so God, I hope I can collect my due.
What will You say, God?
When the Lord calls your name,
will you comply,
or will you try to tell a lie?
Of course, it's futile to tell a lie.
It's written in the Book.
If you don't believe it,
I'm' sure the Lord will let you take a look.
You need to read,
you don't have all day to find the way.
What will You say, God?

For all those who have hurt me,
rejected me,
crushed my heart, caused me pain,
and conspired against me;
for those who wished me failure,
and did their best to discredit me,
I do not hold contempt.
I turned it all over to God.
It is God's call, not mine.
Who knows what angels you entertain?

God works in mysterious ways.
I am His servant.
Be careful whom you lame.
God will judge you.
Will you be humble when He calls your name?
What will You say, God?

One thing I know for sure,
I cannot live without You.
There is no will or way.
What do they say,
"Mine is not to wonder why,
but to do or die?"
No one can do anything without pay.
Isn't that sad that it is that way?
Let me do my part, with an open heart.
Let me live clean and free.
Let me shout for the highest mountain top,
of thy works and omnipotence decree,
given with glee,
and all for me.
What will You say, God?

God, with my limited abilities,
I cannot compete.
I was not given the capacity to review eternity.
All I know is I must live
by love, trust, faith and abide with charity.
I must endeavor to establish my true identity.
I will abide.
I want Your guidance, dear Lord,
I want You on my side.
What will You say, God?

What did you do?
How did you contribute?

Did you give your 10%,
or did you keep God's part?
Do you have a guilt free heart?
What will You say, God?

Did you not see the handwriting on the wall,
which told of the great fall?
Oh God, I pray that I have not been greedy,
nd though my body is tired and weak,
I hope that You have always found my hands out,
helping the needy.
May I have served You well.
May I have been worthy,
and avoided hell.
How do I know for sure?
I do not have the power to foretell.
I stand at Your judgment, and mercy,
and hope that I have done well.
What will You say, God?

Are we just characters in a play?
Do we act out the plot?
What are we trying to convey?
Do we step on the stage, and dance and twirl,
just to entertain someone in another world?
What do You see, God?
What do You foretell?
Are we on Your team,
or are we on the train to hell?
I don't know, God.
I won't know until act III.
Will there be applauses,
will there be an encore?
I will have to wait and see.
Oh, God, have mercy on me.
Hold me tightly, and love me dearly.

I don't know the answer.
I can't see clearly.
What will You say, God?

I'm old and tired.
I have run the race.
I can't go back and erase any of my mistakes.
It's done.
It's over, I had my time.
I surely hope it wasn't in vain.
Thank You God,
You let me live life's full cycle;
a 360 degree rotation.
Many things happened along the way,
as You walked with me in Your reign.
I'll wait for You at the river's edge;
hold my hand as we cross the bridge.
What will You say, God?

Oh, what jubilations it will be on that great sun shiny day!
We will all meet, and dance, and sing, and hug, and love.
It was all foretold in the heavens above.
Oh, what a day of celebration!
What will You say, God?

Did I follow with rage,
or did I behave?
Did I hearken to the call,
or did I stumble and fall?
Did I play in the light,
or did I follow the darkness of the night?
I pray God that I learned nothing to despite.
Oh, God, I stand in need. I cannot go back.
I cannot change one little thought, or deed.
When my story unfolds,
will I be put out to pasture,

or will I be included in the fowl?
Oh, God, bless my soul.
What will You say, God?

Habits are formed.
Habits are traits that are hard to break.
Be careful when you find that you are performing a rite.
It is easy, and you don't have to concentrate.
You just do it.
It is easy as eating cake,
but in the end, your life,
it can break.
Be careful of the habits that you make.
What will You say, God?

God, jump into my boat.
Don't leave me alone,
just to float.
Help me paddle hard;
give me the strength.
Help me to the other shore.
Help me to forget all the trials and tribulations that I bore.
Help me to be born again.
Help me to see Your reign.
Help me above all my suffering and pain.
Help me, Lord, hold my hand,
although I do not understand.
You alone, know my heart.
You know I will never depart.
You are my savior.
What will You say, God?

I want to come home. It's too hard.
I can't compete.
I'm tired,
and I'm weak.

I feel like I have reached my peak.
I give up.
Am I compelled to drink from the cup?
Has Jesus not paid for my sins?
Will You leave me below,
or will You pull me up?
God, will You help me?
Do You see my needs?
I'm at ebbs' low.
I don't know where to go.
What will You say, God?

In my garden, my roses grew,
You knew just what they needed.
You knew what to do.
You gave us seasons, four.
There was never a bore.
Why did I think You should explain
all the things that would keep me safe and sane?
I don't know, I can't retain.
I just know of suffering and pain.
I must hold on, even by a thread.
I can't give in to fright and dread.
There is so much ahead.
Do you believe in what you've read?
It's God that I love and glorify.
I will trust Him beyond the day I die.
What will You say, God?

Was I street lame,
or did I know the ropes of the game?
Was I aware of fair and unfair,
or did I take everything to mean the same?
Did I make a difference of what I did, or how I felt?
Was I mean and immoral? Did I hit below the belt?
What will You say, God?

You know the number of each bird's feathers.
You know me thought,
and through.
You know my heart,
and each little thought that races in my head.
You know each smile I have smiled,
and every tear that I have shed.
You know everything.
How do You know?
Do You record?
Do You keep a record?
Of course, You do.
It is written in the Book of Life.
Please help me to be discreet.
Of my many sins,
I do not want to repeat.
What will You say, God?

Sometimes, I made my bed soft,
sometimes, I made my bed hard.
It depended upon my mood.
Sometimes, I was glad,
sometimes, I was mad,
but You stood by me no matter my state of existence.
What a loving God You are, and what am I?
At my best, I am a child of resistance.
I knew what to,
but I didn't carry through.
What will You say, God?

When my little pets lost their lives, and went away,
I thought that I would never see another bright day.
My friend said to me,
"Who do you think you are
that you can have pleasure without pain?"
I never thought of it that way.

God gives, and God takes.
God knows what He is doing.
I will abide for I am His child.
I only see under the cloud;
God see from the top.
I will go on and on,
for only God knows when it is time to stop.
What will You say, God?

I lived my life so fast, and now,
I regret that part of my past.
I wished that I had loved more deeply,
hugged more often,
breathed more relaxed,
touched when I could,
and accepted all my gifts with gratitude.
Take time to reveal your feelings to others.
Act when you can;
hold back when you should.
Make your surroundings a place of peace and good.
I wish that I had served more diligently,
listened more intensely, and spoken with a softer tone.
I wish that I could have seen more clearly, and
tolerated circumstances more patiently.
All the things that I have wished for,
I was taught, I just ignored the rules.
I went on with my life,
and in some ways, acted like a fool.
What will You say, God?

One day soon, I will come to You.
I will see You face to face.
And on that day—
What will You say, God?